THE CONSULTING ECONOMY

THE

CONSULTING

ECONOMY

HOW TO MANAGE YOUR CAREER
IN THE COMING WORKFORCE REVOLUTION

JONATHAN DISON

THE CONSULTING ECONOMY
How to Manage Your Career in the
Coming Workforce Revolution

ISBN   978-1-61961-609-7 *Hardcover*
       978-1-61961-607-3 *Paperback*
       978-1-61961-608-0 *Ebook*

LIONCREST
PUBLISHING

This book is dedicated to my parents.

The only reason for any success in my life is due to the support and confidence I've had to try, fail, and bounce back.

I hope this book gives other people the confidence to make the leap into consulting or contracting and improve their lives.

Thanks for everything.

CONTENTS

FOREWORD

BY TUCKER MAX, COFOUNDER
OF BOOK IN A BOX

———

In the future, everyone is going to work for themselves.

And that future is already here, it's just unevenly distributed. Consider the following facts:

According to Princeton University research, between 2005 and 2015, all net U.S. job growth was in temporary, part-time, freelance, and other contract or "contingent" work.

According to McKinsey Consulting, right now more than one in three U.S. workers are freelancers of some sort—a figure expected to grow to 40 percent or more by 2020.

According to MBO Partners, in 2012, there were 16.9 million independent workers in the United States. They forecast that number to rise to 23 million in 2017, and project it will reach 65-70 million, or about 50 percent of the U.S. workforce, by 2020.

This is not an accident. Companies are intentionally trying to keep as much of their workforce as possible as external and contract or freelance based and to have the fewest possible full time staff.

Why?

Money, of course.

Having a large portion of your workforce as freelance or contract gets them two things:

1. Lower total labor costs
2. Variable labor costs

It costs a lot of money to hire someone to work full time. The salary is the bulk of the cost, but there are also payroll taxes, health care costs, company benefits, and other assorted costs. For many companies, especially large corporations, the cost of a full time employee is at least 1.3 times, up to 2 times (or more in extreme cases), their salary.

That means if a corporation pays someone $100k a year in salary, the true cost of that employee is $130k to $200k to the company. Hiring contractors cuts those ancillary costs substantially.

But for most companies, the real benefit is in creating a variable labor cost workforce.

A "variable labor cost workforce" is just a fancy way of saying that a company wants the flexibility to only pay for the labor they need to meet the current customer demand. Instead of having a "fixed" amount of labor cost each month (because all your employees are full time), businesses can alter the labor cost to exactly meet the workload they have. In theory, this eliminates paying people who aren't doing anything.

Jonathan asked me to write this foreword because I started a business that is built on exactly this premise—our model works because we are able to use a variable labor cost formula to both maximize profits and maximize quality.

My company is called Book In A Box, and we help people turn their ideas into books. We have a proprietary interview process that allows someone to cut the time they spend writing a book from 1,000+ hours to about 50 hours, all on the phone. We do this by basically combining modern technology and world-class writing talent. We are basically scribes (and we do all the publishing and distribution as well).

Here's where variable labor cost comes in: each book takes about nine different people to work on it, and each one has to be very skilled in their specific task. And though we are doing very well as a business, our work flow is very "chunky"—authors come in waves. We'll sign fifty in one month, and twenty-five in the next month.

To handle this, we have a full time staff of about 20, and then a pool of about 150 freelancers we use to both supplement and augment our full time staff. This allows us immense flexibility in terms of how much work we can handle, what kind of work we can take on, and who we can serve.

So what? Why does this matter to you?

The model my company uses is going to become the predominant employment model for most corporations. Meaning, you are probably going to run your business this way eventually, or you will probably become a contractor (if you aren't already).

Yes, this applies to you. It doesn't matter what industry you are in. It doesn't matter what you do.

In fact, on net, it will usually benefit you. In *every* industry, the best and brightest are realizing that they can usually make more money and have more freedom if they are contractors instead of full time workers.

The only question for you now is do you make the shift consciously and intentionally to maximize the upside for yourself, or do you ignore this inevitable megatrend and then struggle to adapt when it's too late?

And that's the thing about this shift that almost everyone in the press is missing, and you may be too:

This is a good thing for everyone.

To explain why, let's go back to my company as an example:

A common mistake is to think that the "gig economy" is relegated to lower-level workers, like Uber drivers or Upwork freelancers. This is not the case. In fact, the gig economy is not just low-end labor.

My company has access to a wide array of highly talented people. We routinely work with Emmy- and Pulitzer Prize-winning writers on a contract basis. We could never afford to hire these people full time (nor would we want to because of our chunky demand), nor would many of them want to work with us full time, but they love working with us on short, one-off contracts.

Why?

Because they can essentially monetize their downtime. We pay well and our process is such that they can use the work we provide to fill in their free time, or the time they don't have high-paying gigs (if they don't have a full time job). The work they do with us is fairly simple (for them), but they enjoy it, and are good at, and they know when it will begin and end, so they can use it exactly the way they want.

We clearly benefit as a company because we get access to high-level talent for a fair rate.

The author benefits because they get access to the same high-level talent, without having to pay a premium price or find this person and manage the process.

Everyone in this interaction wins.

There are so many perks to this non-full time employee arrangement for contractors:

1. **Contractors get freedom.** Are you tired of a bad boss, going to an office you hate, or the same grind every day? Doing contract work is an amazing solution. You get to pick who you work for, what you will do, and how much you get paid.
2. **Contractors can often get paid** *more.* We pay our high-level free-lancers very well, usually very close (or even more in some cases) to what they make at their full time job, or what they make on their "big" projects. Think about it: If a company has to spend a total of $200k a year to employ you, they will spend anything less than that to hire you as a contractor. So if your salary is $125k, you can charge them $160k for a one-year project, and you both come out much better off on a per-dollar basis.

This is coming to corporate America in a big way. In fact, it is already here. So what do you do now?

This is where Jonathan Dison comes in.

Jonathan has worked in the consulting industry his whole career. He knows the industry inside and out, but unlike most management consultants, he is a businessman and entrepreneur. He has real skin in the game, and he has proven his abilities in the market. He not only started his own successful consulting firm (LightRock Consulting), but he also started his own software company to help consultants (BenchWatch).

He is the one who connected all of these dots for me, and he wrote this book to help you understand the exact same thing. This book will show you:

1. the change that is coming, and why it's inevitable;
2. how this change can be good for you, if you manage it well; and
3. most importantly, how you thrive in this new world.

My grandfather used to tell me that there are no safe places, there are only safe people. In the future world of business, Jonathan is one of the people who can help you stay safe.

Listen to him.

HOW TO NAVIGATE THIS BOOK

This book has two objectives:

1. Convince you to become an independent consultant or contractor
2. Help you execute

The first two chapters are dedicated to educating you on the industry and the opportunity for you, and the remaining chapters focus on the tactics of helping you execute and be successful.

Chapter 1 is meant to convince you of the huge opportunity in this industry. People frequently misunderstand what *consulting* or *contracting* is, and they think it isn't for them.

Our first job is to reset your understanding and convince you that clients are already looking for you.

Chapter 2 is meant to speak to your specific stage of life: early career, mid-career, late career, or semi-retirement. Each of these phases is uniquely different and presents different hurdles and opportunities. Again, here we continue to attempt to convince you of the opportunity. If you aren't convinced by this point in the book, you can stop reading, because it's not worth your time. If you are convinced, the rest of the book gives you tactical advice on how to execute.

Chapter 3 helps you with the "mental shift" of being a consultant. First, you need to think of yourself as a business. Second, you need to have a service mindset. Both of these can be difficult for people, especially if they've had a "regular" employee job for their entire career. But in making this shift, you'll feel personally empowered and thrilled by your work in a way you never have.

Chapter 4 helps you with the tactics of setting up your business. This can be a time-consuming process if you don't know what to do. We've been through it all and know all of the answers. For example, the best business entity structure for an independent consultant is an LLC (limited liability company) that functions as an S-corp (simple corporation). It provides the simplest administrative burden (almost zero) while protecting your personal assets. This chapter should save you a lot of time and headache.

Chapter 5 helps you land projects. It's all about helping you market yourself in a way that saves you time and money. There are some very good nuggets of information in here that will save you a lot of time and effort. For example, we help you carve off your niche and develop the perfect résumé that helps clients feel confident hiring you.

Chapter 6 provides some additional tips and tricks I've learned: things like how to become indispensable as a consultant, so clients rehire you. Or, different tax-savings tricks that are unique to being a consultant.

Additionally, this book is meant to be an active guide that you refer back to as much as needed throughout your journey as a consultant. Therefore, the table of contents has been designed as a quick reference guide specific enough to help you quickly find topics you want to review again.

INTRODUCTION

The contents of this book stem from a single conversation. A conversation I've had *hundreds* of times with different professionals. It's the conversation in which I convince them that not only are they capable of being a successful consultant, they're capable of doing it *today*.

For some reason, people don't see the opportunity or have the confidence to jump into it. This book is your guide to the consulting industry, and your blueprint to navigating without fear.

Let me start with a story...

One of my early hires at my consulting firm was a woman who'd never consulted. My firm specializes in servicing the energy sector—and she'd never worked in that world either. She didn't have a business degree, an economics degree, a background in finance, or any of the certifications that signal "consultant."

In fact, the only relevant experience she had was as a project manager at a big company (Fortune 500). I'd met her years before, when I was hired on as a consultant by her company. She was my client, and we worked together to execute a company-wide implementation of a new technology. She was smart and hardworking, and though she had a reputation as a "bulldog," we got along very well.

A few years after we worked together, she called me after she'd been let go when her company downsized. She had worked there for twenty-two years, she loved the company and her job, and now it was over. She was in bad shape.

I immediately asked if she'd come work with me. Her response is something I've heard hundreds of times: "I can't do consulting—that's not for me. Why would anyone pay me to 'consult' them?"

I told her, "Look, I need people on this project who: (1) have project management skills; (2) have strong communication skills; (3) I can trust; and (4) care about doing a great job for the client. Do you have those things? I know you do, because I've seen them. They aren't hiring consultants to run their company, they're hiring consultants to execute a project—a project I've literally executed with you before."

She reluctantly took the job. Mainly because she'd be working with me, and believed I'd "protect her." But I knew she'd be fine.

That project was at Chevron, a Fortune 500 company. In other words, this wasn't some rinky-dink company—this was the major leagues.

Since that conversation, she's been rehired for projects at Chevron for over five years (at the publishing of this book she's still there). She's never had one hour of downtime, she makes more money than she ever did at her old company, the client loves her, she owns multiple houses in multiple states, and she has the freedom of being an independent consultant. She's happier and more fulfilled by her work than at any point in her career.

This isn't a story about how I took some young professional under my wing and mentored them to success. *I didn't teach her any new skills.* I just opened her eyes to the opportunity of consulting, something she'd never considered, even though she was more than qualified.

In other words, I gave her confidence in skills *she already had.*

I've found this to be true with so many professionals. They think the only path forward in life is to become a full time employee of a successful corporation and slowly grind their way up the ladder. What they don't realize is that they are uniquely positioned to take advantage of the most important economic macrotrend of the next decade: the exploding market for independent consultants and contractors.

STOP THINKING "I CAN'T BE A CONSULTANT"

The most common question I hear about consulting is, "What does a consultant actually do?"

There's probably not another major industry so opaque that the general public is confused about what a professional actually does in it, and that's not by accident. Major consulting firms have spent over 100 years operating behind a curtain. Clients hire them to solve a problem or help with a change, the firm recommends and/or implements a solution, and they move onto the next contract. In the past, clients didn't have visibility into the firm's internal processes, but that's changing.

This dynamic has created an image of consultants as the smartest guys in the room. If a company has a problem, they hire a consulting firm, and it is magically fixed. From the outside looking in, it makes it seem like consulting firms are composed of business prodigies who understand the high-level strategy behind every business.

In reality, maybe 5 percent of the work consultants are hired to do involves helping clients with their higher-level strategy. *Ninety-five percent of the time consultants are hired, they're just there because they have the skills to execute a client's project, and the client doesn't want to hire full time employees to do it.*

If you're a professional with a single marketable skill—project execution, change management, expertise with specific software, communication or marketing, accounting or finance—you can be an independent consultant taking home up to $400,000 a year, instead of an employee trading your time for a salary at a corporation.

YOU WILL NEVER HAVE SUCH A GREAT OPPORTUNITY AGAIN

Full time employment is a dying trend. If you're a professional now, in the near future you will have no choice but to become an independent contractor (for the sake of this book, *contractor* and *consultant* are interchangeable terms).

I'm going to talk about this in greater depth later in the book, but the most simple explanation is this: companies have realized that it makes more sense to outsource the bulk of their work to an external workforce of consultants and contractors who they pay on a project-by-project basis, as opposed to hiring full time, salaried employees for every project.

For example, it is much more affordable for a company to hire one salaried IT Director who oversees all technology for the company, and then hire a team of consultants whenever they have a new IT project, like implementing new software. Relying on contractors for project execution, the company only ever pays exactly as much as they need to get the job done. No bloated payrolls, no need for a dozen managers.

The consultants they hire to implement new software aren't going to be MBAs who specialize in mergers and acquisitions, they're going to be people who previously would have worked in IT for a large corporation. Now, instead of being professionals who trade their time for money to one single corporation, those IT experts get to be consultants, who bill at a higher rate per project for multiple clients. Both parties—the IT consultants and the company—benefit from this approach and make more money.

This trend has been building for several years but is accelerating now, and the demand for consultants with specialized skills is skyrocketing. Eventually the market will force most professionals to become a consultant or contractor, but right now you have a chance to get there first. If you move to capitalize on your opportunity and become a consultant before the rest of the world, you'll have a massive advantage.

If you're reading this book, you are ahead of the game, while everyone else is still searching. Years from now, you'll have competition, but for now, you have a path to success no one else knows about.

The key is to move now.

BECOMING A BUSINESS

The best decision I made in my life—besides marrying my wife—was to become my own business.

I started my career at Arthur Andersen, which was one of the most prestigious consulting firms in the world. I remember walking into the office in downtown Houston on my first day, fresh out of undergrad, and being blown away. The office was on one of the top floors of the most high-class building in Houston. The entire office was dark wood and had recently been recognized in the magazine *Architectural Digest*.

It was fancy. But that wasn't the only thing that struck me. The office was full of expensive things, but there was one thing noticeably missing: **people.** There were literally only a few people in the office.

I understood then, on my first day, why being my own business made sense. Consultants don't work in their office, they work in their client's office. The firm doesn't pay their salary, the client does. I realized in that moment that the firm was just a matchmaker, connecting me to the clients that needed my skills. I was the one providing value, and apparently I was providing so much that the firm could afford an opulent office that approximately zero consultants used.

I didn't have the courage or the tools to go out on my own at that point in my career, and Arthur Andersen was renowned for their ability to develop their talent. I spent the next six years at Arthur Andersen learning the ropes, building my network, and acquiring the tools to eventually break out on my own.

When I finally did, I realized I had to learn an entirely new set of skills. I knew how to service a business, but now I had to learn how to *be* a business. Over the years, as I learned and developed, I found more personal and financial success than I could have imagined. Eventually, I had so much work I had to create a consulting firm and hire other consultants to give it to.

However, instead of hiring full time consultants and paying them a salary, I hired independent consultants like me. I hired them on contract, then connected them with my clients. By charging a slight markup on their bill rate (much lower than a traditional consulting firm), everyone in the transaction—the client, the consultant, and the firm—makes more money.

I believe so strongly that this is the future, I've even invented software to make it easier for independent consultants to get hired. My company, BenchWatch, allows consultants to create a profile listing their skill set, bill rate, and availability and uses patent-pending trust technology to connect them with consulting and staffing firms searching for contractors.

The more professionals who move toward being independent consultants, the better it is for everyone. Companies pay less for more specialized talent, professionals make more than they would through a salary, and consulting firms like mine bring in revenue without paying for a full time staff.

There is a problem, though: the transition to this world is hard. There's a whole lot of knowledge required to go from being a salaried professional to being an independent business. You have to understand the market for your skills, the ins and outs of running a business, the keys to marketing yourself as a consultant, and most importantly, you have to truly understand the economic landscape that is creating this opportunity.

That's why I wrote this book, to lay out a blueprint for any professional ready to go out on their own and become an independent consultant.

CHAPTER 1

THE OPPORTUNITY

———

The consulting industry is one of the largest, fastest-growing industries on the planet. Let me put this into context: if you combined the NFL, NBA, MLB, and NHL, they would equal around $147 billion in revenue—roughly one-third of the $425 billion consulting industry.

Conservative estimates by the U.S. Bureau of Labor predict that the consulting industry will grow 6 percent yearly over the next five years. I believe strongly that those numbers aren't just low, they're *infinitesimal* compared with reality.

The consulting industry is going to grow *at least* twice as fast.

There are three key reasons for this:

1. Companies are rapidly shifting to **flexible workforce solutions** in which the majority of their work is handled by contractors while a small core of full time employees oversee the company.
2. Smaller, specialized firms that hire experienced professionals as independent consultants are disrupting traditional behemoth firms who hire mostly MBAs as salaried employees.
3. Technology is making it easier than ever for independent consultants to be connected with clients.

To really understand how this all works, you need to understand modern consulting.

CONSULTING REDEFINED FOR THE TWENTY-FIRST CENTURY

There is a lot of confusion around the terms *consulting* and *contracting*. If you Google *contractor*, you'll find mostly ads for construction companies, because that's the industry we associate the term with.

Likewise, if you Google *consultant*, one of the first results you'll see is for Bain & Company, one of the largest management consulting firms in the world. When we think of the term *consultant*, we think of high-priced management consultants, whispering advice to CEOs in closed offices.

The reality is that neither of these definitions is correct. A consultant and a contractor are the same thing in functional terms. They are each a professional who, instead of working for a company full time, works on contract for clients. That's it.

Uber, TaskRabbit, FancyHands, and whatever other gig economy apps you use in your life are a reflection of this dynamic. Every Uber driver you've ever had is a contractor. When we're talking about lower-skill jobs, like driving a car, we call workers members of the "gig economy." When we talk about professional services, I call it the "consulting economy."

This is key to understanding modern consulting. The consulting industry isn't growing at a historic rate because big firms are getting bigger—they're actually dying. The consulting industry is getting bigger because **professionals from every industry are becoming consultants.**

In the very near future, **nearly all professionals will be consultants or contractors.**

If you understand what is powering this change, how you can benefit from it, and how you need to navigate the new market, then you can position yourself to take advantage of the greatest opportunity of your professional life.

WHY THIS IS HAPPENING NOW

On a very basic level, the reason for the growth of the consulting industry is simple: companies need more consultants and contractors, in a wider variety of roles, than ever before. This is true and obvious to anyone in the corporate world.

However, to really understand the pace at which the consulting industry is growing, you need to understand a greater economic trend.

For the last seventy or so years, your professional career was defined by your company. You started off at an entry-level position and worked your way up.

You didn't trade services for money, you traded time. Your company signed you to a full time deal, gave you a salary, and you gave them your time in return. This model worked very well for a long time, and helped create a lot of America's prosperity in the twentieth century.

But that same model has stopped working for companies for a number of reasons:

1. **The pace of change has accelerated.** It is well known that business moves faster now than at any time in history—and this is only increasing with new technology and evolving market forces.

Companies need much more flexibility and nimbleness to be able to adapt and thrive.

2. **Bloated workforces cripple a company's finances.** With the traditional full time model, companies cannot expand and contract to meet demand. A company's workforce, and therefore personnel costs, remain static, while their revenue fluctuates.

3. **Firing full time employees is expensive.** One of our clients recently had to let go of over 1,000 employees. Each of those employees received *twelve months* of salary as part of their severance package. That high price tag makes it very hard for companies to be flexible and adapt their workforce to their needs.

To achieve the adaptability that the traditional full time employee model prevents, companies are turning to flexible workforce solutions. These are solutions that run most of a company's operations through a team of contractors or consultants, while a small core of full time employees oversees the entire company.

This transition is changing the makeup of the workforce. Companies in the near future are going to have very few full time employees but will need access to a lot of consultants. In turn, professionals who today are full time employees at different companies and firms are almost all going to be private contractors or consultants.

WHO WINS AND LOSES IN THIS NEW WORLD

Consulting is a centuries-old, $425 billion industry. Like any industry of that size and age, there are several major firms that have historically dominated the market:

→ McKinsey & Company
→ Boston Consulting Group
→ Bain & Company
→ Accenture
→ IBM
→ Deloitte

And many more. All of these firms have thousands of employees, with offices in virtually every major city worldwide. They service all the biggest corporations in the world, and they employ graduates from the top MBA programs.

And they're all in trouble.

Smaller, specialized firms that contract consultants as independent businesses instead of salaried employees are disrupting the industry. These firms have been on the rise for years now and are taking over the consulting market. Small firms offer access to better talent at a lower price and are more geared toward the industry-specific needs of a business.

This isn't a theory of how the consulting industry might someday be disrupted; it is an observation that consulting is absolutely being disrupted right now, as we speak. If you want to understand why smaller firms of independent consultants are rising up to dominate the industry, you have to understand how transparency has affected the industry.

HOW TRANSPARENCY GAVE RISE TO THE SMALL FIRM

The consulting industry has been opaque for over a century. Consultants work within a "black box" where clients only see the output, not the process that led to it. If the clients don't like the results, it's difficult for them to see where things went wrong, and even if they do ultimately decide it was the firm's fault, there's never been a central repository for them to review their experience.

Think about it: if you had a bad time at a restaurant, you could write a review on Yelp! If you had a bad experience with BCG, where would you broadcast that information?

This has left clients in a particularly challenging situation where they:

1. don't know exactly what a given firm does behind the scenes—just that they claim to deliver results;

2. don't have any way to review a firm's quality; and
3. have to judge a firm by their prestige.

This dynamic has allowed giant firms to get away with severely overcharging clients. For example, if you hired a major firm for a marketing project, you might meet with one partner at the firm who is an expert in marketing for your industry and feel confident about their ability to deliver for you.

Then, when you sign your contract with the firm, they'll use a technique we call "backing up the bus." This is where a firm unloads a huge team of junior consultants on your project, each of whom gets paid around $50 an hour, and bill you $150 an hour. The consultants are usually just a year or two removed from their MBA and likely have no particular expertise in your industry. However, because you don't see what goes on behind the scenes and have no basis for comparison, you have to accept that this is the way things go.

Thankfully, this is changing. Clients for the first time are being selective about which firms they use for which projects, and instead of hiring one giant firm to do everything, they're hiring smaller, specialized firms for specific tasks.

There are two things driving this change:

1. Financial strains post-2008 have forced executives to interrogate their bottom lines and demand transparency from firms that charge exorbitant fees.
2. Massive turnover rates among major firms have lead to more ex-consultants working for corporations. With their intimate knowledge of consulting firms, they make much more informed decisions about which firms they work with.

The second point is really critical to understand. The turnover rate among major consulting firms is about 20 percent, meaning there are tens of thousands of ex-consultants out in the workforce working full time for corporations.

When the companies those alumni land at hire consulting firms, those ex-consultants are valuable information resources. They know what a given firm is actually good at and what they are not suited for. They know when a big firm is trying to "back up the bus" or play games with them. Even more importantly, they know the difference between a high talent level and a high bill rate.

Equipped with the information to make good decisions, they'll typically hire smaller, specialized firms like ours, where they get more talent at a lower cost.

Clearly, it makes sense from the client's perspective to work with independent consultants, but the advantages are just as massive—if not more so—for the consultants themselves.

CHAPTER 2

WHY CONSULTING IS GREAT AT ANY STAGE IN YOUR CAREER

———

The most frustrating question I hear is "Am I qualified to be a consultant?"

The short answer is "Yes." Everyone is qualified to be a consultant, and the only question is which consulting jobs you are qualified for.

If you have a deep understanding of Office 365, SAP, Salesforce.com, or other big technologies and have implemented them at your company, you can become a consultant and land contracts at major companies. If you have strong communication skills, you could work for a large corporation as a communications consultant. Just having an expert-level knowledge of Excel and SharePoint can qualify you to take a consulting job at many companies.

Of course, higher-level strategic skills like change management or expertise in mergers and acquisitions are also highly marketable consulting skills, but the majority of consultants don't have these traditional management consulting skills. Instead, they have one thing they do really well that companies have need for.

Any skill or proficiency you have that a company would need qualifies you to be a consultant.

If you are good at—or even interested in becoming good at—any particular skill, consulting is the right move for you. Whether you're just starting off, in the middle of your career, or looking to retire, consulting presents a world of benefits.

EARLY CAREER: GET PAID TO LEARN

Deciding to become a consultant early in one's career is a no-lose proposition. Even if you are the most junior person on the job, you will be exposed to the nuts and bolts of how change happens in an organization. The experience will put you well ahead of a peer who leaves school and takes a limited, entry-level position. For a graduate who is unsure about a career direction, consulting provides the ideal opportunity to learn skills and experience that are applicable to any field.

Becoming an independent consultant fresh out of college may seem risky, but based on my experience, the demand mitigates the risk. I have worked at companies where 40 percent of the workforce is external. Most Fortune 500 companies have between 100 and 300 projects going on at any given time. Assuming that the top 2,000 companies worldwide have on average 200 active jobs, each with five to ten contractors, the opportunity is huge. And this doesn't even include non-Fortune 500 large companies or midsized companies. The market is massive, $425 billion per year and growing.

Most projects typically last six to twelve months, which offers a relatively stable base of income and minimizes risk. In addition, many companies are regularly looking for junior people with low billing rates to fill out the ranks of their workforce on a short-term basis.

Having a lower hourly rate is a big asset for a young consultant. When you are young, the opportunity to acquire experience is far more valuable than making a lot of money, and billing rates should reflect that fact. With a few projects under your belt, you can slowly raise your rates.

A $25 hourly fee will make anyone extremely attractive to prospective clients. A willingness to travel or live in other locations will also set one apart from competitors in the marketplace.

This is great, because hirers can get great value out of you, while you get the one thing you should care about right now: **experience.**

Your entire goal when you're first starting off should be to develop the skills and connections to have a viable consulting career. This means doing a lot of old-fashioned networking, being hungry, and taking on tedious grunt work just to be exposed to bigger projects.

At this point in your career, you probably aren't going to have a résumé that will blow people away. Maybe you've achieved a lot relative to your age, but still, in comparison to a consultant who has been succeeding in the industry for twenty-five years, you simply won't have the track record.

Many young people in this position think that the best move for them is to pursue an MBA. In 2014, the MBA became the most popular graduate degree in America for the first time, and it's easy to see why. People are desperate for the magic bullet that will take them to the next level professionally, and they've been raised to believe that a higher degree or certification is that bullet. Among those graduate degrees and certifications, the MBA—the degree of CEOs and investment bankers—reigns supreme as the perceived highest-valued degree.

This explains the rise of Executive MBA programs, marketed to working students who are willing to take weekend classes and carry severe debt for the promise of brighter prospects.

The problem is, **an MBA has no guaranteed return.** In fact, a recent study found that nearly two out of three recruiters believed MBA programs do a poor job of preparing students for their careers.

In my humble opinion, the only time you should pursue an MBA is if you get into Harvard or a program of that stature. The very top programs, such as Harvard, Wharton, UChicago, still carry a large ROI. Other programs just carry a large price tag.

If you're looking to enhance your job prospects, you don't necessarily need an MBA. What you need is experience delivering the only thing the market cares about—**results.**

You can do this in a lot of ways. A lot of people are taking unpaid or pro bono positions to gather experience. Others are finding entry-level roles with low salaries. All of these strategies can work, but in my opinion, require unnecessary sacrifice.

You can make a good living and acquire the experience you need to move forward by becoming an independent consultant. As an independent contractor, you can in a sense create your own MBA from the experience you gain and get paid very well while doing it.

CREATE YOUR OWN MBA WITH CONSULTING

Years ago, I met a twenty-five-year-old kid while on a project. He worked in a junior role at a company I consulted for—nothing fancy, more or less a plug-and-play role that required him to show up and grind—and he made a good impression. He was competent, hardworking, and enjoyable to talk to.

Honestly, that in and of itself isn't very impressive. Spend enough time around successful companies and you'll meet a lot of talented staff; they're the backbone of good business.

What set this person apart was his initiative. He did whatever he could to learn more and gain experience—not by pestering anyone, but by volunteering to help out wherever possible.

At some point, we developed a good rapport, and we were close enough that he felt comfortable asking me for career advice. He was considering going to a local university for an MBA.

I told him not to. Rather, I told him to come work for my firm or any other consulting firm.

He didn't have any expert-level skills, and he wasn't incredibly knowledgeable about any industry, but he had a **deep hunger and hustle** and **a low bill rate.**

As a young person getting into consulting or contracting, those are your two greatest assets.

Two months later, I was putting together a team of consultants for a project, and I told the client I had a utility player who could work under me and get things done for $60 an hour. Compared to the $180+ hourly bill rate they paid for other consultants, bringing him on was a no-brainer.

He was put on a twelve-month contract at one of the largest companies in the world, taking home around $70,000 a year (and they felt like he was a bargain).

The salary was great for him, but the biggest reward he got was the experience. He learned new skills, he learned the industry, and he got to put a Fortune 500 company on his résumé.

He makes well into the six figures now, and that early experience is the reason why.

You can do the same thing that twenty-five-year-old did no matter where you are in your career, you just have to know how. You can break the process down into four steps:

1. Get Your Undergraduate Degree

Right now it's trendy to advise against going to college at all, even for an undergraduate degree. If you're going to drop out of Harvard to invent Facebook, then go ahead, but otherwise you need an undergraduate degree.

Pick something you're interested in that has some market application. You don't have to major in business or finance, but if you decide to major in poetry, you better be sure it somehow corresponds to your niche (marketing or communications, for example). Hard science majors are always valued, of course.

Think of your undergraduate degree as a driver's license. You need a driver's license to be able to drive to and from the office, but you don't get extra points for having one. Similarly, an undergraduate degree doesn't guarantee anything, but it's the minimum ante to get in the game.

2. Articulate Your Niche

Clients can only trust you if they know exactly what you can and can't do for them. They won't hire you because you seem generally competent; they have to know exactly what they're getting.

Your niche doesn't have to be high-level strategy for Fortune 500 companies. Too often, people who have never been in the consulting world believe that unless you can directly advise the CEO, you can't be a consultant or contractor.

Your niche can be as simple as being really good at accounting. Companies don't need an army of strategic advisors, but they do need a huge cast of roleplayers who can execute specific skills. What's the one skill you can consistently execute for a client?

Once you have your niche, frame your résumé around it. List your key skills that support your niche, and highlight all of your past experience that underscores your ability to execute in that niche.

3. Set Up Your Business

This is the critical step if you want to make money. Registering yourself as an independent business takes about an hour with LegalZoom, and it opens the door to a huge income increase for you.

If you're an independent consultant, and you're contracted by a firm for a project, you don't make a flat salary. You charge an hourly bill rate, and the firm marks that up to the client. So if you charge us $30 an hour, and the firm marks you up to $50 an hour, clients are thrilled to be paying less than the usual $150+ consultants charge, you make over $60,000 a year, and the firm makes a nice profit.

On top of that, you get all of the tax breaks that come along with being an independent business. Your cars, your technology, even dinners and office space in your home can be written off as a business expense.

4. Find a Firm That Will Mentor You

The key benefit to an MBA is that you learn about business from experts. Imagine how much more you would learn from an expert who is *currently in the field.*

If you work for the right firm, you get to contract with consultants and contractors who are at the top of their industry and learn directly from them by being part of their team. Also, because you are an independent business, you aren't obligated to work for only one firm.

You can be a part of multiple teams—that's the whole concept of a "bench" in BenchWatch—and learn from multiple mentors.

Instead of coursework meant to simulate real business scenarios, you'll actually be in real business scenarios, and you'll have a team of experienced consultants around you to help guide you through.

A lot of people never make the jump into consulting for the same reason they decide to pursue an MBA without really evaluating their decision. **They fear uncertainty.**

People are afraid they won't land projects, that they'll land at a firm they can't grow with, or that they simply aren't good enough. More importantly, they haven't seen enough other people take this path to know for certain that it is viable.

If you're experiencing these same hesitations, understand two things:

1. **You don't have to give up everything to start consulting or contracting.** You can start off slow by doing work on nights and weekends. Once you are confident, you can expand.
2. **There are more consulting opportunities than you think.** Consulting and contracting as an industry is worth over $425 billion, and as more companies transition to contractor-centric workforces, the opportunities are only increasing.

Your chances of going into consulting and landing no contracts is incredibly low. It requires less investment of capital than a new degree or certification, and it carries a higher potential reward. The choice is really very simple.

MIDCAREER: MAKE YOUR JOB SUPPORT THE BUSIEST TIME OF YOUR LIFE

In your twenties, you thought you had a handle on retirement, or at least an idea of how everything would play out.

Honestly, compared to where you are now, were you *even close* back then?

There's no shame in missing the projections you made in your early twenties. You didn't know anything then— none of us did! The truth is, this is the first time in your life where you can honestly reflect in a meaningful way. For the first time:

1. You've made big moves in your career.
2. You've learned who you are and what you want.
3. Even if you don't have a family, you've built a life bigger than your job.

Although all of these things are great and represent growth, they also give way to a new kind of fear.

When you were younger, you were worried because you couldn't imagine how things would go. Now, you can imagine exactly how things will go—**and you feel powerless.**

Maybe you aren't going to hit retirement at the age you wanted. Maybe you don't see yourself reaching the level you wanted in your career. Maybe you can't see a future in which you have time for your family and career ambitions.

It's this fear that drives people to enroll in an Executive MBA program, or start shopping their résumé around to different companies—even though they'll likely end up in an identical position.

What you actually want in this situation is control, and the best way to get it is by becoming a consultant.

HOW CONSULTING GIVES YOU BACK CONTROL AND STABILITY

One of our great pleasures at LightRock Consulting has been working with professionals on a variety of different courses in life. Because all of our consultants are independent businesses, not salaried employees, any professional can work with us and take as many clients as they can handle.

For someone in their midcareer who is struggling to take back control, this is the ideal arrangement. Let me give you an example.

One of the consultants we work with is a working parent. At thirty-five, her career was doing well, but she had a conflict between her professional ambitions and her need to be around her kids. She had enough experience to be realistic about her situation, and if she remained in her current job, she had two choices:

1. Sacrifice time with her children to grind and reach the professional level she wanted

2. Sacrifice productivity—and therefore promotions—for more time with her children

That's a brutal conundrum to find yourself in, and it's one an incredible amount of middle-aged professionals experience.

What she didn't realize then—and what she found out later—is that she had a third choice. By setting herself up as an independent business and contracting with clients through LightRock, she gets to dictate the terms of her career.

She works a full time schedule because she wants to, but she gets to have hard-and-fast rules for areas such as:

→ when she does and doesn't work during the day,
→ her availability for travel,
→ her bill rate.

She doesn't have to work during the periods of time she wants to dedicate to her children, she doesn't have to travel and spend time away from them, and she gets to charge more than she did as a full time employee—and raise her rate as she gains experience, not when her boss says it's OK.

She can hit her retirement goals, reach the heights she wants in her career, spend time with her children, and, most importantly, she can do it all on her terms.

She's just one example. We've worked with professionals who just felt stuck in their careers or who loved their jobs but wanted to make more money. The point is, they were all able to live their life on their terms, without compromise, because they took up consulting.

LATE CAREER: MONETIZE YOUR EXPERIENCE AND RELATIONSHIPS

Your fifties are when you cash out as a consultant. You've spent the last thirty years making a living, but also making connections and building experience. You've reached the point in your career where those assets are at their maximum value, and they allow you to make a huge jump.

Think of it this way. If you're a full time employee at fifty, and you've worked with your company since you were twenty-two, you have twenty-eight years of experience doing what you do. That makes you an expert.

However, **your pay at your company isn't tied to your expertise.** It's tied to what you made at forty-eight, and that pay is tied to what you made at forty-six, and so on.

As a consultant, you have access to a world of clients who need an expert for one specific project. They don't look at your bill rate as an increase in payroll; they look at it as a one-time expense to be calculated into their margins.

If you charge $200 an hour, your clients won't think "We can't raise our payroll by over $400,000 a year for this guy." They think "Over 6 months, this contractor will cost us $288,000, and the resulting project will bring in millions of revenue for us year in and year out long after the contract ends."

That math makes a lot more sense from a client's perspective, which makes them willing to pay out for top-tier talent, and as a fifty-year-old professional, you have the experience to justify that price tag.

The other thing to keep in mind is this: all those professionals you built relationships with in your twenties—the ones who were five or ten years older than you—are now presidents, CEOs, or major project leaders. They're in positions where they can make buying decisions, and your relationship and skills make you their ideal candidate.

SEMIRETIREMENT: WORK ON YOUR TERMS
AND NEVER STRESS ABOUT MONEY

For those of you old enough to have to care, retirement planning is a bear. Even when you've saved enough to meet whatever projections your financial planner laid out for you, there are still a host of fears you must deal with:

→ What if the markets crash again?
→ What if I outlive my savings?
→ What if my living expenses change drastically?

These fears are very real and very well founded no matter what sector you work in.

The average American family has $5,000 in retirement savings, according to the Economic Policy Institute. Government pensions, whose perceived security has long been a major selling point of positions in the private sector, are underfunded by tens of billions of dollars and are facing crisis. Millions of people who'd saved their whole lives for retirement lost everything when the 2008 recession hit and crashed the funds they'd invested in.

Everyone is looking for a safety net, *and that's exactly what consulting is.* If you're worried about retirement, start building your consulting résumé now. Embracing semiretirement through consulting will stabilize your retirement, alleviate your fears, and in many cases allow you to live a fuller and richer life. There are three main reasons for this, each of which I've broken down in this chapter.

MARKETS CHANGE; SKILLS DON'T

Retirement savings are usually tied to the market in some capacity. The Great Recession of 2008 crashed those markets, reducing the value of many retirement funds. On top of that, the widespread and sudden shrinking of the job market led to mass layoffs, which left many people unemployed and forced them to take money out of their shrinking retirement funds—often at a penalty.

Even now, almost a decade removed from the crash, we can see how a small change in the market can fundamentally change a person's retirement reality. When Illinois reduced the expected return on their pension investment from 7.5 percent to 7 percent, it lowered retirement savings for government employees so much that taxpayers had to pay an extra $400+ million to cover the difference.

Although markets can be volatile, your skill and experience don't fluctuate.

If you're set up as an independent business, and you know that you can find plenty of work billing at above $150 an hour, how much do you really have to worry about running out of money in retirement?

I know so many retirees whose retirement savings cover their basic expenses, but consult on short-term contracts for supplemental income. They don't have any stress about their retirement savings not being enough, because they know they can go make more money whenever they want.

Their lives are stress-free, they are financially positioned to do whatever they want, and all it took was for them to put together a consulting résumé and reach out to their network.

WORK AS MUCH AS YOU WANT

According to The Pew Research Center, more Americans are working past the age of 65 than ever before—and the trend is only increasing.

One of the biggest fears Americans approaching retirement have, one which is obviously founded in reality, is that they will have to work full time until the day they die. In other words, they question how "semi" semiretirement actually is.

The fact is, with consulting, you can escape the binary of being fully retired or fully employed. One of the many rewards a career in consulting offers is **the ability to set your own hours,** which is one of the reasons it is a perfect part-time career for working parents or young people with other full time jobs.

As a retiree, you don't want to work forty hours a week. That's the entire point of retirement. But if you could bill $200 an hour, how many hours a week would you need to work to make enough to support your retirement?

I'm willing to bet it's fewer than you would work taking on a full time job.

RETIREMENT ISN'T THE END

There's an aspect of retirement we never talk about, because it touches on some pretty fundamental fears we all hold. As much as we look forward to an easy life, to enjoying what we've spent our lives saving for, there's a real darkness to saying, "I'm taking myself out of the race now. I'm going to go relax until I die."

Obviously, not everyone feels that way, but a significant portion of people do, and because of that, retirement terrifies them. If you're a person who enjoys work, then retirement—especially forced retirement—is truly scary.

Consulting is the perfect option for you if you fall in this category. You don't have to find a beach to live on or take up a random hobby to fill your time. You can still work, at a pace that fits your lifestyle, and continue to grow and keep your hands busy.

My own father is the perfect example of this. He loves business. Loves being involved in big decisions, in executing projects, in working with other people. Relegating himself to a country club full time would be a nightmare for him.

At seventy years old, he's still working, still sharp, and loving every bit of his life.

When we talk about retirement, we have a tendency to do so as if retirement means giving up our agency. We either have enough money saved up to live a comfortable, uneventful existence, or we have to work a full time job till we die.

With consulting, this dilemma is nonexistent. Are you scared of completely quitting on your career? With consulting, you can stay involved. Are you worried you won't have enough money? You can always make more as a consultant. Are you scared of working full time in retirement? You can consult one day a week.

You have options; you just have to get started as a consultant. You can do it yourself by learning how to set up your consulting business, define your niche, and market yourself, or you can use a done-for-you service like mine to get yourself set up as consultant immediately.

CHAPTER 3

THE CONCEPTUAL SHIFT TO BECOMING A CONSULTANT

Consulting requires you to rethink a lot of your basic assumptions about work and your career. The consultant's mentality is both an owner's and a servant's mindset, and understanding this duality requires some explanation.

The aim of this chapter is to help you understand the basic conceptual shifts you'll have to make to succeed as a consultant, including the following:

1. You are a business.
2. You define success for you.
3. You must have a service mindset.

Let's start with the idea of becoming a business—and why you should be thrilled about it.

YOU ARE A BUSINESS

There's a lot of confusion about what it means to be an independent business, because people have a tendency to overcomplicate it. You've almost certainly done business with people who were independent businesses before, you just didn't realize it.

Let me unpack this. In the past, you've almost certainly been part of an **employee-employer relationship.** You've worked full time for one company, trading your time for a salary.

In the consulting economy, however, the standard employer-employee relationship is gone. In its place is the **client-contractor relationship,** in which professionals like you operate as independent businesses, servicing as many companies (clients) as they like.

This shift should seem familiar to you, at least as a client. We talked about this earlier in the book, but if you've ever called an Uber or hired a TaskRabbit, you've been on the client side of the contractor relationship (although most people would call this the "gig economy," the basic idea is the same).

Services like Uber and TaskRabbit are just the beginning. The change is only going to get bigger, and it's going to expand to other parts of the economy, like professionals. In fact, as the individual economy grows, *most professionals*—lawyers, accountants, consultants, and so on—are going to be independent businesses.

A lot of professionals are afraid of this change. I disagree. Professionals should be excited. If you are a professionals, this is the best thing to ever happen to you. Being a business means you have more control, make more money, find work more easily, and enjoy greater stability than you ever did as an employee.

YOU'RE ABOUT TO MAKE A LOT MORE MONEY

If you are an employee taking a regular salary, you're leaving money on the table. To see what I mean, don't think about your monthly take-home, think about how your salary maps to your hours worked. If you're salaried, your hours don't change your pay, meaning the more you work the less you earn per hour.

However, if you are an independent consultant or contractor, you set your own bill rate and hours worked. The firm that connects you to your client will take some percentage, but your billed hours still translate directly to your income.

You work more, you make more. It's that simple.

The other financial benefit to being an independent business is the money you save on taxes. The entire U.S. tax code is built to incentivize business ownership. There is no better way to lower the amount you pay in taxes, and keep more money, than to start your own business. As a full time employee (as I'm sure you're painfully aware), all of your income is taxed. If you make $250,000, you pay taxes on $250,000.

As a business, however, your business expenses are not taxed. If your business makes $250,000, but you invested $150,000 of that back into the business (in the form of office rent, business meals, travel, etc.), you only pay income taxes on $100,000 that remains.

What makes this amazing for you is that when you're a business, you can include business purchases that also benefit your personal life in your write-offs. This includes:

→ office space in your home (effectively tax free rental income to you),
→ cars (when you use them for business),
→ technology (computers, TVs, phones, wireless routers, iPads, etc.),
→ business-related dinners, and
→ business-related travel.

The steep discount the government gives on these business expenses is the single greatest tax benefit you'll find.

YOU CAN BE A BUSINESS AND BE STABLE

I understand why you might be nervous about giving up your full time job. Full time, in our world, has always meant the same thing as "stable." The world is unpredictable, and having a dependable salary, benefits, a 401(k), and guaranteed severance pay if things go wrong is a huge safety net. Or at least, it has been.

Let's dispel this notion of being an independent as "unstable." Looking at the advantages of full time employment mentioned here, it becomes clear that they fit neatly into two categories:

1. **Advantages that save money.** Employer-sponsored benefits are widely seen as cheaper than buying your own insurance.
2. **Advantages that help you sleep.** 401(k)s and guaranteed severance pay lets you know that no matter what happens down the road, you'll be OK.

Starting with the second category, are you sure full time employment is guaranteeing your future? Right now, a higher percentage of people over sixty-five are still working compared with any other time in the past half century.

Is the severance pay guarantee worth making significantly less for your work? Why not just save up the money you make as an independent consultant, and use that as a fund for when things go wrong?

As an independent business, you set your own bill rate, you set up your own retirement savings (which, all things being equal, will likely be better than anything your current employer offers), and you save an incredible amount of money in taxes.

The extra money you make on your hours billed and on your taxes will more than cover the cost of buying your own insurance, and this way, you'll also have the option of buying the insurance perfect for you and your family.

In my opinion, more money equals more stability, and being your own business almost always means more money.

You'll also notice that finding clients is much easier than finding open full time positions, because modern companies actually want you to be an independent business.

WHY COMPANIES WANT YOU TO BE A BUSINESS

This is where a lot of professionals get hung up. They can see the upside to being their own business, but they can't see why a company would want a contractor instead of a salaried employee.

Let's use consulting firms themselves as an example in this exercise. Think of the situation from a firm's perspective. If the firm is paying you a consistent salary, then the cost (and risk) you represent to them doesn't change. If they bill a client 200 or 10 hours for you in a month, you cost them the same amount of money.

Every single consultant the firm brings on as a full time employee is, to some degree, a financial burden to the firm. If the firm suddenly loses work, they have to pay severance, lay people off, and deal with the expensive inconvenience of downsizing.

Alternatively, if the firm brings on a bunch of new work, they have to weigh stretching their current workforce thin versus hiring a bunch of new talent they might not need in six months. This exact situation happens to all companies who use full time employees, not just consulting firms.

Simply put, full time employees make it impossible to be flexible. That's why most consulting firms have adopted flexible workforce solutions.

Firms can scale on demand now, hiring consultants as needed and paying them on a project-to-project basis. If you're looking for work as a consultant or contractor, it's actually going to be *harder* for you if you're not an independent business.

However, all of these benefits are worthless to you if you can't define success for yourself.

YOU DEFINE SUCCESS FOR YOU

In the context of the thirty-year job, there is really only one version of success. You grind long enough to slowly climb the ladder, and you end your career somewhere relatively high in the company with a good salary and retirement savings.

As we've discussed previously, the thirty-year job is dead, and as a result, so is that version of success. One of the hallmarks of a career in consulting is its flexibility: you pick your hours, your clients, your specialization, and most importantly, your trajectory. Depending on where you are in life and what you want most, your version of success is going to vary wildly from another person's.

We talked in Chapter 2 about why consulting is great for anyone at any stage of their career, and how you should define success according to your career timeline. To recap, here is a quick overview:

→ **Early career (twenties):** Your entire goal here is to gain valuable experience and relationships. Make enough money to survive off more than ramen, but don't worry too much about cracking six figures in your first few years.

→ **Midcareer (thirties and forties):** This is the time in your life where you set very specific goals for the next twenty years and build a life that accommodates all of them. If you need more money for retirement, this means taking on more clients. If you need more time with your kids, this means setting a firm schedule that still meets your career ambitions.

→ **Late career (fifties):** Now is the time to make as much money as possible. You're perfectly positioned as far as experience and relationships to start cashing in, so raise your bill rate and start taking on the most expensive projects you possibly can.

→ **Semiretirement (sixties and later):** This is all about enjoying your life. Work as much as you have to to feel both fulfilled and financially secure, while maintaining the freedom to enjoy your retirement.

This is the general blueprint to defining success for yourself. However, there are other considerations you must take into account. How you define success for yourself is going to heavily rely on what you choose to prioritize in your life. In figuring out your priorities, it's helpful to ask yourself the following questions:

→ Do I want more time to myself, or do I want to make more money?

→ Do I have other people dependent on me right now?

→ Do I value stability and security, or do I value flexibility and independence?

→ Am I comfortable with my current lifestyle, or do I plan on upgrading or downgrading?

→ Do I enjoy travel, or do I prefer to stay stationary?

→ Do I draw energy from working on a team, or do I prefer to work alone?

→ Am I a natural manager, or do I prefer to have a clearly defined role?

All of these questions will help you define the balances you'll have to strike to find success on your terms.

YOU MUST HAVE A SERVICE MINDSET

If you ask young MBAs who want to become consultants why they picked this career path, a lot of them would say the salary. There's nothing wrong with that. Everyone likes making money, and consulting can be a lucrative profession, so it may seem counterintuitive that the greatest motivator for truly successful consultants is *not* money.

It's the joy of service.

All clients love a "service mindset." This includes you. When you are the client—whether it's at a restaurant or car mechanic—you notice and appreciate being well taken care of.

What will a service mindset do for you?

1. **It makes you more influential.** When you're clearly motivated and have a service mindset, your motives are in the right place. Clients feel this and inherently trust you.
2. **It makes you love your job.** When you understand that a client is buying *you*, they become sacred. You feel validated and confident, and become even better at your job. Being appreciated is one of life's true joys.
3. **Clients buy trust and positivity.** More than anything else, clients want to work with people they enjoy and trust. If you earn this reputation, clients will rehire you over and over.

Every aspect of a consultant's job lends itself naturally to servant leadership. If you can learn to channel that, you can take yourself to the next level.

There's nothing greater you can do for your career as a consultant or contractor than demonstrate service to your client. This skill will pay off multiple times for you.

WHY COMPANIES CRAVE SERVANT LEADERS

Servant leaders aim to empower others and create value for their team. I'll give you a very simple but powerful example: Not long ago, a contractor at our firm was hired to lead a team on a new project. The work was difficult and deadlines were tight. When we got feedback from the client, they mentioned this leader's willingness to always do the little things to help others. They mentioned getting coffee and helping prepare for meetings by making copies. This was a highly paid consultant in a leadership position, and this is what stood out to the client...getting coffee.

That is servant leadership.

Think about the leaders that stand out in your mind. Is it their genius that stands out, or is it the little things they did to help you or others succeed or feel good? If you are religious, think about the "servant leaders" that shaped the history of your religion. Did they give orders, or did they demonstrate leadership through service?

This mindset is literally magic and will ensure your success. If you focus on helping your client (and team) instead of yourself, you will be wildly successful.

It's very hard for companies to get this from full time employees. Companies owe employees a career path and career development (which is expensive and time-consuming). In a way, the company works for the employee.

CHAPTER 4

GET STARTED FAST AND EASY

Years ago, setting up a business was a hassle. You needed a whole team of professionals including attorneys and financial advisors just to get off the ground. On top of that, the initial startup costs associated with buying technology and setting up an office—mobile technology wasn't nearly as advanced as it is now—were huge and intimidating.

Now, you can set up a business, complete with legal documentation, sophisticated accounting systems, and a bank account and line of credit for your business, all in twenty-four hours. Technology has created one-click solutions to processes that previously required warm bodies and weeks of lead time.

One of the keys to success in any business is knowing when to get out of your own way and hire someone to do something you're not good at. If you have an oil and gas company that needs fixing, I'm a good option for your situation. If you have a Mercedes that needs fixing, I am nowhere near up to the task. In fact, if I tried to help you with your car, there's a big chance I'd make it worse and set you up for frustrations later.

The same is true for setting up a business. If you're a business attorney who has set up dozens of businesses for clients, by all means, go ahead and draw up all the paperwork to your exact specifications. If you don't have that experience, however, just use LegalZoom.

LegalZoom provides legal services online at a low cost. Using it, you can set up your entire business in a few quick steps.

CREATE THE CORRECT BUSINESS ENTITY

Your business entity is the structure or type of company you register your business as. There are several options here, each with different legal implications regarding earning distribution and taxes. The most common options are:

→ sole proprietorships,

→ partnerships,

→ corporations,

→ S corporations, and

→ limited liability companies (LLCs).

When you set up a business through LegalZoom, the first thing the software will ask you under "Business Formation" will be how you want to classify your business entity. You can research this separately if you'd like, but after setting up dozens of companies, we can say for certain that as an independent consultant you want to set up an LLC and **elect to have it taxed as an S corporation.**

If you want to know the reasoning behind this, I've explained it in detail in the following text. Otherwise, feel free to read ahead.

On a very simple level, the reason for setting your business up this way is that an LLC is the most administratively low-maintenance business structure you can have, and an S corporation provides significant tax benefits. If that's all you need to know, move on to the next chapter. If you want a more in depth explanation, read on.

An LLC is a simple business setup under which owners are protected against liability over their personal investment in the company (hence the term *limited liability*). In practice, this means that if you invested $15,000 in your LLC, and the company took on $50,000 in debt from creditors, you would only be liable for $15,000 even if your company failed.

LLCs are in general the business formation with the least red tape. They require less sophisticated reporting than other business entities, and they will not face quite the same level of legal scrutiny as other types of corporations.

LLCs also "pass through" their profits directly to their owners' income tax, meaning that if you are a one-person business, all the profits you make in your business are reported as personal income and taxed normally. This is not what you want, hence the need to be taxed as an S corp.

A Subchapter S (S corporation) is a form of corporation that meets specific Internal Revenue Code requirements, giving a corporation with 100 shareholders or less the benefit of incorporation while being taxed as a partnership.

In a larger C corporation, the business pays its owners a salary, which they report on their income tax. It then pays out dividends to its shareholders, which are taxed at a lower rate (much lower when compared to higher income brackets). As an independent business, this means you can pay yourself a lower salary that avoids a higher tax bracket, while paying yourself the difference in dividends that are taxed at a low rate.

However, larger C corporations are taxed as independent taxpayers, meaning that before you get your salary or your dividends, that money has already been taxed once. This is where the phrase "double taxation" comes from. S corporations are not taxed as independent taxpayers, meaning you get the benefit of the corporate tax structure, while avoiding double taxation.

SET UP YOUR BUSINESS BANK ACCOUNT

Keeping your personal finances separate from your business finances is mandatory. In the event of an IRS audit, the last you thing you want is a convoluted financial record. You want it to be clear-cut and as simple as possible.

The key to doing this is to set up a separate bank account for your business. To register a bank account for your business, you need your business to have a **Federal Tax Identification Number.** This is a nine-digit number which identifies your business to the IRS.

If you register your business through LegalZoom, you will have the option of letting them issue a Federal Tax

Identification Number for you, which I'd recommend you do.

As for picking which bank you set your account up with, this is going to depend a lot on your preference. As a general rule, talk to a number of different banks and feel out whether or not they are a good fit for you. There are simple things to look for, like which bank has a better fee structure and which bank you can negotiate the best deal with, but then there are more complex factors to take into account.

For instance, are you going to stay a one-person business for the foreseeable future? Because if you have plans to take on other consultants in your business, you're going to have to talk to your bank about running payroll—unless you run payroll through a different service.

PICK THE RIGHT INSURANCE (HEALTH AND BUSINESS)

Insurance is a complicated subject, and it's one with strong emotional ties to the majority of professionals—especially in America. Next, I've broken things up into two sections, one dedicated to picking the right health insurance, and the other to picking your business insurance.

Let's start with your health.

HOW TO CHOOSE THE RIGHT HEALTH INSURANCE

At this point in American history, the health insurance world is in flux, and so this section will not focus so much on individual plans, but instead on the overall mental shift you need to make when it comes to insurance and where you get it.

One of the biggest fears professionals have about jumping into consulting is their loss of insurance. I talk to professionals all the time who hate their job, who see the clear benefit of transitioning to consulting, but can't do it because they're terrified of losing their employer-sponsored insurance.

Here's the big problem with this mindset. If you think you can't leave your job because your employer is paying for your insurance, you are completely misunderstanding your relationship to your job. **Your employer isn't paying your insurance, you are—it's why your salary is lower than it should be.**

The only time you should be afraid of losing employer-sponsored benefits is when you're quitting your full time, W2 position for another full time, W2 position. In the interim, you will not be paid, because you will be unemployed, and so will be unable to afford insurance.

However, if you're jumping into consulting, then income isn't a concern for you. We've already covered that you're going to make more money as a consultant than you did as a salaried employee. That income increase will more than cover the cost of your private insurance.

You have to understand insurance from a business owner's mindset, not an employee's. Insurance is a business expense (and a tax deductible one at that), not a supplementary form of income.

It's easier to make this mental shift when you see the monetary upside to thinking of insurance this way. As a W2 employee, you'll probably make between 20 percent and 25 percent less than you will as an independent consultant. The employer-sponsored insurance you're afraid to lose will cost you maybe $400 a month to replace on your own (though this varies by factors such as age, geographical region, and number of people covered).

I've worked with consultants who have left over $500,000 on the table over a ten-year period because they waited to make the switch to being an independent business. They could have insured themselves, their family, and a more than a few friends with that much money.

HOW TO PICK THE RIGHT BUSINESS INSURANCE

Liability insurance for your company is a non-negotiable part of business. Clients aren't going to hire you on unless they're insured against damages (for example, crashing your car into a company vehicle) and crime.

Luckily, this is incredibly simple. Although your specific insurance needs are going to vary depending on your industry and clientele, in general you want at least $1,000,000 in general liability insurance and $250,000 of insurance against crime.

After shopping around an incredible amount insurance providers, we've found Hiscox, an online insurance seller, to be the best in terms of price. Because they operate online with a low overhead, they're able to offer insurance at extremely low rates.

SIMPLE TIME TRACKING, INVOICING, AND ACCOUNTING

Some companies will provide their own time tracking and invoicing software, and in that case, you obviously should use whatever they recommend. However, in many cases, clients are going to count on you to handle the invoicing and accounting side of things.

We have used most of the popular time tracking, invoicing, and account software, and the one piece of software we've stuck with is FreshBooks. It allows us to track our time easily, it automatically handles invoicing, and it connects with our business credit card to create detailed expense reports without us manually entering anything. It becomes an entire accounting system for our company, and it only costs around $40 a month. Also, because it's cloud-based, we are able to access it from any device we happen to be using.

As an independent consultant, you want the simplest system that fits your needs. In the majority of cases, FreshBooks is going to be that.

PICKING THE RIGHT BUSINESS CREDIT CARD

Every independent business needs a credit card that feeds directly into their business bank account and integrates into their accounting system. There are obvious metrics to compare cards, like interest rates, but the perks of specific credit cards can also be differentiating factors.

After trying almost every credit card, I've settled on two that I prefer. I recommend the American Express Platinum card to businesses that do a lot of traveling, and the American Express Green card for those who don't.

Aside from their rates, it's their perks that make them so useful. For example, I get deals on flights, upgrades, and access to members' lounges because of my company's Platinum card. That may not seem like a big deal, but when you fly as much as we do, it's incredible.

If you don't travel, the Green card is cheaper. Both cards offer protection on rental cars and other benefits that help your business.

There are other considerations to take, like handling your insurance and benefit plan, but these are the bare-essential steps to getting your business off the ground. Once your business is officially set up, you can think about growing it.

OTHER USEFUL TOOLS FOR CONSULTANTS

Although things like a business credit card or accounting software are obviously critical needs for any independent consulting company, there are a variety of consulting tools that you might not think about—tools that are actually incredibly useful.

I've put together a short list of these tools, in no particular order:

1. **Your own computer.** Previously, clients would give you a laptop to use that was already integrated with their systems. However, as everything has moved to the cloud, most clients have adopted a "bring your own device" policy. Although most devices are compatible, you generally want a device that natively supports standard business software, like Microsoft Office. We recommend the IBM ThinkPad, and the Microsoft Surface.

2. **Software registrations.** You need to have a business account for major business software, like Microsoft's Office 365. This software suite comes with all of the standard Office applications (Word, PowerPoint, Excel, etc.), as well as Microsoft's cloud file system, OneDrive.

3. **A notebook.** Carrying the classic black and red notebook around might seem trivial to you, but walking into a meeting carrying it makes you look more professional and gives you something to easily take notes on. You won't believe the difference this makes in how people interact with you.

4. **Headphones.** Headphones are lifesavers when you're working with a client whose office is incredibly noisy. (Trust me, this will happen to you.) We recommend headphones that can easily fit into your pocket or laptop bag, like the Apple AirPods or Bose noise-canceling headphones.

CHAPTER 5

HOW TO MARKET YOURSELF AND GET FOUND

———

Marketing yourself is the key to finding work as an independent consultant. It used to be, for most consultants, the hardest part of their job. The goal of this chapter is to make this once-difficult process easy for you by providing a blueprint for success.

Marketing yourself and finding work independently is a huge mental shift for professionals. You don't have a boss assigning you work anymore. Instead, you have to think like a business owner and bring clients to you.

There are two key pieces to this:

1. Defining your niche
2. Marketing yourself: basic, intermediate and advanced

In this chapter, we're going to take the mystery and guesswork out of this process. There is a straightforward blueprint to carving off your niche and marketing your services that you can follow to find clients, and we're going to break it down into easy, actionable steps, starting with defining your niche.

CARVE OFF YOUR NICHE

Understanding how to carve off your niche as a consultant is difficult, but critical for your success. I learned this lesson the hard way and want to save you some pain. Early in my career, when I was first starting my consulting firm, one of my partners got us a meeting with an executive at Hewlett Packard. We walked into the HP offices and listed every service and skill set we could think of: business transformation, mergers and acquisitions, process optimization, technology implementations—we essentially told them everything we could do (and more).

I was confident we'd landed him as a client—after all, we had a trusted relationship and we told him we could do anything they needed. But as we walked out, this executive gave me one of the biggest lessons of my career: "You guys are telling us you can do everything, *and we know that's not true.* We want to know what you can do better than anyone else."

What he was saying was that we didn't have a niche. We didn't get any work—and we learned a hard lesson. We thought listing more skills would help ensure we hit on something they needed, but that wasn't true at all.

That conversation taught me that less is more, and that for consultants there is hardly anything more important than carving off your niche.

WHY NO ONE WANTS A CONSULTANT WHO DOES EVERYTHING

To be an effective consultant, you need to understand where you fit in a company.

People who do everything, who wear ten different hats, manage multiple departments, and have their hands in everything a company does should be part of a company's full time core team.

Consultants, on the other hand, are hired to execute in a specific area. You have one piece of a project to manage, one objective to achieve. If you aren't clearly articulating why you're the best for their one specific need, a company has no reason to hire you.

Plainly put: generalists don't get hired—specialists do. Your other skills will allow you to help the client in other ways and possibly grow your role. But to get hired, they need to match you with a box they need to fill.

Another way to think about this is trust. If you're new to a client, they need to be able to "put you in a box." When your skills and experience neatly match a role they need, they're much more likely to trust that hiring you will work than if you're ambiguously "good at everything."

Psychologically, this is because trust is about risk assessment. Dr. David DeSteno found in a recent study that in all relationships, trust requires one party to expose themselves to the other.

This vulnerability is easier when one party knows exactly how the other party is going to behave. In other words, if you're an unknown quantity, you pose a much greater risk and are therefore harder to trust.

All hiring is about trust. If you can define your niche and articulate your skills well, you will build trust. If you build trust, you will get work.

So how do you do that? How do you find your niche, so you can build trust? The first step is auditing yourself.

HOW TO AUDIT YOURSELF AND FIND YOUR NICHE

Auditing yourself starts with asking the following questions.

1. What Do I Love?

It's a fact of life that you will do better if you specialize in a field you love.

This might seem strange, but I love the oil and gas industry. I enjoy reading and learning about it. And because I enjoy it, I understand the context and challenges of the industry.

I also enjoy "being in the trenches" of a project. I like planning, executing, learning what's working, fixing things that aren't, and seeing a project through to completion. I actually enjoy this so much that I still execute projects at my consulting firm, rather than step back and sell more work.

This "niche clarity" is the single most important reason our firm has grown. Clients know what we are good at. And when they need it, they call us. And if their coworker needs it, they recommend us.

What are you interested in and good at? Think back to classes that you've taken, projects you've worked on, books you've read. Among your favorites, what is the common theme? It could be a particular skill like project management, or it could be a field like the oil and gas industry.

Quite frankly, ask yourself, "What do I like, or even better love, doing at work?"

2. How Can I Create Value at Work out of What I Love?

If I loved the oil and gas industry, but could only channel that passion into oil painting, I wouldn't be creating any real value for companies like Chevron. You need to put a frame on your interests and skills that make them relevant to the people hiring you.

If you're passionate about a field, frame that interest around a skill you possess:

→ If you're a strong writer who loves the auto industry, say you specialize in communications for automakers.

→ If you love technology, pick two or three that are relevant to most businesses (Office365, Salesforce, SharePoint, etc.) and say you're an expert in implementing or managing them.

→ If you really enjoy planning and executing projects, organizing all the details, and working with groups of people, talk about your focus on project management.

The key here is to find the vocabulary to translate your passion into a skill a company would want.

Once you've done that, you have to point to places in your past where you've actually used that skill. You have to prove you have it.

3. What Experience Can I Reference?

Most people are unaware of how experienced they are. We have a tendency to see our experience with a very narrow view.

The reality is, you probably have a ton of relevant experience, but you just don't understand how to frame it. To figure out how to frame your experience, do this:

→ Make a list of every project (or change) you've worked on and every role you've held.

→ For every project or position, breakdown the skills and technologies you learned. Pick the ones you want to be your niche.

→ List any experience related to your niche and leave out anything that's not related.

Don't add any jobs that you think are impressive but aren't relevant. Keep your résumé entirely focused on the skills you're articulating, and be prepared to talk about your experience.

BUT WHAT IF I DON'T HAVE ANY EXPERIENCE?

A lot of young people legitimately don't have experience yet. If that's you, it's OK. Following are some thoughts to consider, based on my experience hiring hundreds of consultants and contractors.

1. If You Have a Little Experience, Focus on Passion

Showcase your passion for the project. If we're looking at two applicants for a position, and Applicant A has more experience than Applicant B, but Applicant B says something like, "I've only worked on a few projects like this, but I loved them for these reasons and I want to make a career out of them," we're going with Applicant B.

I know that even though they have less experience, they're going to absorb information faster and work harder than the other applicant. Passion goes a long way in predicting success.

2. If You Have No Experience, Trade Money to Gain Experience

When you are young, nothing is more valuable than experience. Please note, I said *experience*, not education. Don't go spend $50,000 to get a master's degree. Take any job you can get that gets you the experience you want.

To make it easy to hire you, drop your compensation as low as needed to get the job. And make this clear to the hiring manager. Here is a statement that can't be ignored: "This is what I want to do with my career, so I really want to gain experience in this area. I'm willing to drop my compensation to make this an easy decision for you. What compensation makes that happen?"

If you say that to me, you are hired. I understand your interest, your passion, and you are cheap. In general, people want to help others (especially young people), so if you make it clear and easy, they will hire you.

In the long run, you will more than recover the money, because you'll have experience that you can monetize.

BASIC MARKETING: RESUME, BENCHWATCH, AND LINKEDIN

You can break your marketing up into three tiers: basic, intermediate, and advanced. This section is dedicated to the place we all begin in, the basic phase.

At the basic level, all you're trying to do is create some visibility for yourself in the professional world. Visibility isn't at the core of hiring, but it's a necessary first step. You can't get hired if no one can find you.

For 70 percent of people, this stage is all the marketing they will ever need. You can do just this and make in the six-figure range.

What a lot of people get wrong about making themselves visible is that they misunderstand the goal. Your objective isn't to get your face in front of as many people as possible, it's to **get in front of the right people—in this case, employers.**

There are three key things you'll need to do this right:

1. **A LinkedIn profile.** LinkedIn is the professional Facebook. It's not the best tool to figure out if you can really trust someone, but it's great for increasing your visibility.

2. **A BenchWatch profile.** BenchWatch gets you consulting jobs by making your availability, skills, résumé, and bill rate available to staffing firms and clients looking to hire consultants and contractors.
3. **A résumé.** Your résumé becomes a sort of "fact sheet" for hiring managers to reference when they're debating which candidate to hire. It's a critical first impression. Don't worry, we can help you build the perfect consulting résumé.

Before we move any further, we want to share some advice on writing a résumé as a consultant. I've looked at thousands of résumés, and the best have the same structure:

→ At the top of your résumé, define your niche in two or three short sentences.
→ Beneath those sentences, note three to five top skills with bullet points.
→ Under skills, list experience. Detail projects you worked on and skills you acquired.
→ After experience, cover any testimonials or related press coverage you've had.
→ Finally, talk about your education. This is far and away the least important detail, and people tend to overemphasize it.

INTERMEDIATE MARKETING: PERSONAL WEBSITE, BLOG, AND ARTICLES

Visibility is great, but it is only the starting point, and frankly, very few consultants ever move beyond that stage. But it's only the beginning.

Once you're visible, the key to leveling up is to prove you are a high-quality candidate who has done the work before. You want to prove that you have the initiative to succeed and that other people have trust in you.

To this end, the next three key things to have are:

1. **A personal website.** Having your own site gives you the space to really differentiate yourself. It also proves that you get things done, and truly own your brand as a professional. We recommend using a service like Wix to build your site.

2. **Testimonials.** If an employer trusts somebody, and that person trusts you, that's a big trust signal. Even if you don't have mutual personal connections with a hirer, having someone respected in your niche give you a testimonial on LinkedIn or your résumé is huge. LinkedIn testimonials are great, but what are even better are video testimonials on your personal site.

3. **Demonstrated proof of work.** The more you can show potential employers you have done the exact same thing they are hiring you for, the better.

These three things in tandem elevate you to a higher level professionally. You aren't just some fresh face looking to make your way. You have a professional identity.

If you can have a professional identity, you will be in the top 25 percent of all consultants and have a constant stream of good projects to work on. That's great, and if that is your only ambition, you can stop reading now.

But many consultants want more. They want to level up and move beyond a constant flow of good work, and start being able to pick and choose their jobs and charge high fees for them.

To level up like that, you have to move from a person who belongs to a professional niche to a person who *influences* that niche. Being seen as an influencer or thought leader in a field is a big differentiator to employers, and one that will dramatically increase the amount and quality of work you're offered.

The goal here isn't to prove how well connected you are, but to show that you're more than just good at what you do. You're so knowledgeable about your niche that **you actually help people learn and define trends in your niche.**

The fastest and most effective way to do this is to write and publish articles about your field or niche. Industry reports, editorials on trends you see, advice and guides for others in your field—all of it will help establish you as an industry insider in the eyes of hirers.

If you're not a writer, but you have plenty of insight to add to your field, it's worth hiring a service to turn your ideas into articles for you. There are several you could use, but we recommend using Thought Leader Media, if you decide to go down this road. We have used them ourselves and can vouch for their effectiveness.

You could also use Influence & Co. We have not used them, but know many consultants who have.

ADVANCE MARKETING: BOOK AND SPEAKING ENGAGEMENTS

The final tier is to become the known expert in your niche (or microniche).

When companies are looking for someone to execute a billion dollar project, they don't want to interview ten people who are very good in the space. They want to hire the absolute best, the foremost authority on the subject.

There are many things you can do in service of this goal. You can build a portfolio of experience on bigger projects, you can build a reputation through work and writing, and you can network your way to the most impressive testimonials possible. Those can work.

However, there is only one guaranteed way to become the expert in your field: **write a book.**

You can't just write any book. You have to write *the* book on your subject. The key to achieving this is to be as specific as possible with your focus. You want to go an inch wide and a mile deep.

For example, if you wrote a book on the general topic of business IT, you'd be one of 1,000 authors who'd done so. Writing that book is great, and it will establish your credentials and authority, but it won't make you *the* expert in IT.

But, if you wrote the book on marketing automation in the natural gas industry, you could very easily become the expert on the subject.

The next time a major company decided to bring on a consultant for their most important marketing projects, you'd be their first call.

In this situation, we really recommend you work with a professional to write your book. If you have any writing experience, you can probably write your own articles, but a book is a different beast.

We strongly recommend Book In A Box. Not only are they well established and have worked with hundreds of high-level consultants, they have a process by which they take your actual words and ideas and create a book, as opposed to ghostwriting. Having your book be your ideas and words is key, and they are the only service we know of that does this.

Once you have a book, you can begin the process of booking speaking engagements. There is an art to any sort of PR, but on a basic level, reaching out to various events you'd like to speak at with review copies of your book is a great way to get in the door and start booking speeches.

CHAPTER 6

SECRET TIPS AND LESSONS LEARNED

———

There are a variety of lessons you learn on the job as an independent consultant that you couldn't learn in a classroom. This chapter is a compendium of all the lessons I wish someone had told me when I first made the jump, which I've had to incrementally learn over the years.

LESSON 1: TRUST IS EVERYTHING

It doesn't matter if we're talking about kings appointing generals 1,000 years ago or project leaders hiring consultants today, hiring always comes down to trust.

Why do you think we care about things like references and testimonials? Why do we want to list prestigious companies and universities on our résumés? What difference does it actually make if we're connected to impressive people on LinkedIn?

All of these things *signal that a person can be trusted to deliver.*

The problem most professionals have is that **they fundamentally misunderstand how to create trust,** both with existing and potential clients.

They're taught early in their careers that building a trustworthy reputation is a numbers game—how many C-suite connections can you make on LinkedIn? How many major brands can you fit on your résumé?

The reality is, trust is built one relationship at a time. If you can make one client trust you on the deepest level, they will refer more business to you than 500 executive connections on LinkedIn who vaguely know you.

One of the big mistakes modern professionals make is assuming that technology has made hiring easier. Technology hasn't made it easier to hire for roles, it's made it easier to *apply* for them.

Consulting and staffing firms are constantly flooded with thousands of résumés, because applicants can now apply in a matter of minutes. Similarly, when companies hire a big consulting or staffing firm for a job, the firm can do a simple database search for consultants fitting the job's criteria and e-mail the client hundreds of résumés in an instant.

Having thousands or even hundreds of résumés isn't useful, and it doesn't make hiring any easier. No hirer wants to be in a position where they're considering thirty almost identical résumés, trying to figure out who's the better fit.

What a hirer wants is **the one person they can trust to deliver.** They want a person who has delivered before, for people they trust or admire, and who has the confidence of people the hirer respects.

Once a client has that consultant or contractor they can trust, that relationship is locked in. As long as the consultant maintains that trust, they will get repeat work from that client for the rest of their career.

For that reason, trust is the bedrock of your career as a consultant. If you want work, clients have to trust you will deliver what they need. If you don't know how to cultivate trust, you won't go very far in the field.

There are three things a client needs to trust you:

1. Certainty that you will deliver
2. The belief that you're worth more than your bill rate
3. The ability to articulate their needs to you

Next, I've expanded on each of these ideas in detail, explaining why clients need them to trust you, and how you can best fulfill those needs.

YOU PROVE YOU CAN DELIVER THROUGH REPETITION

Trust is about expectations. When you trust someone you work with, your expectation is that they will deliver the results you need. **A trusted consultant is a dependable one,** and you only prove yourself dependable by delivering over and over again.

Many consultants—especially young consultants—fall into a mental trap around this topic. They believe that because they've only worked junior-level roles, they lack the senior-level track record to land higher contracts. In other words, because they've never been a project manager, they can't prove they are dependable in that role, and therefore cannot be hired for it.

That's a vicious cycle, but thankfully, it's not the reality. **Clients don't gauge your reliability based solely on what roles you've held, but by how well you've delivered in them.** Even if you've only ever done basic admin work for a client, if you delivered over and over again, they're going to trust you as a reliable person, and they will be likely to give you more responsibility.

I can't tell you how many times we've had clients specifically request a consultant who never had more than a junior role for them, just because that person had earned their trust by delivering for them over and over again.

When you try to land a higher contract with a client you've delivered for, they aren't going to say, "That person has only worked on X or Y, we can't hire them for anything else." They're going to remember you as the person who never let them down, as a person they can trust.

CLIENTS TRUST A CONSULTANT WHO OVERDELIVERS

Earlier, I shared a story about ruining my chances with a prospective client by telling them I could do a hundred things for them, when they only wanted me to do one. Part of that story is that I didn't define my niche. I couldn't yet articulate the one specific thing I was the best in the world at.

There is another part of this story, however, that applies to young consultants specifically.

I was overpromising and setting myself up to under-deliver. We see a lot of young consultants and contractors do this, and it makes sense why. You want clients to understand how valuable you are, and so you tell them all the results they could potentially get by working with you.

The problem with promising everything is that even if you deliver everything, *you're only doing the bare minimum.* You've set the expectation so high that absolute perfection is just a passing grade.

If, however, the expectation is set that you're going to deliver something very specific, say a company-wide implementation of new software, you have a chance to overdeliver.

If you finish the project ahead of schedule, set up great training materials for employees, integrate quickly into the team, and actually make the people you work with better, you've delivered what the client wanted and then some.

Here's another way to think of it. In purely financial terms, if a client hires you to a one-year contract that will cost them $220,000 ($110 per hour), and you deliver $300,000 worth of value to them ($150 per hour), they got a great deal. However, if you promised them $1,000,000 worth of value, then it doesn't matter how great their return on investment was with you—you didn't live up to what you promised. They will measure you on the gap between what you delivered and what you promised.

CLEAR LINES OF COMMUNICATION SUSTAIN TRUST

One of the reasons trust is so critical for a consultant or contractor is that trust makes business enjoyable. Anytime someone brings on a consultant, they are taking a risk. If they spend a significant amount of company money and don't deliver results, they're responsible.

Trust takes that stress out of the relationship for the client. They trust you to deliver, and so the perceived risk of hiring a consultant is drastically lowered.

However, trust requires upkeep. As new problems and obstacles arise, clients have to be able to come to you for answers. You can't solve a client's pain if they can't articulate it to you. **If a client is experiencing pain that you can't solve, their trust in you will falter.**

When oil prices fell by 50 percent in 2014–2015, a lot of clients in the energy sector were facing serious challenges.

The procurement groups started aggressively renegotiating with consulting and staffing firms to drive down costs. Firms with trusted relationships and open lines of communication with clients were able to gain insights to understand what the client needed. These firms were able to stay. Those who didn't have open lines of communication were typically cut off completely.

We saw several smart consulting and staffing firms cut their rate by 10 percent to 20 percent without impacting the rate paid to the contractor. Then as oil prices stabilized, the client allowed them to increase rates to recover their profit margin.

LESSON 2: HOW TO BECOME INDISPENSABLE

When you're first starting off as a consultant or contractor, finding work can be a grind (BenchWatch helps a ton!).

You spend that first-year marketing yourself like crazy, just trying to get your foot in the door with companies. Slowly, you start landing projects, start getting referrals, and build relationships with clients that go beyond individual projects.

Then something amazing happens. You get a repeat client. Someone liked working with you so much that they want to do it again.

Then another client rehires you. Then another.

All of a sudden, you have to turn new work away, because you're fully booked with repeat business.

That's the way the consulting industry works. If you do a good job, after a couple of years consulting full time, you can expect over 90 percent of your work to come from repeat clients. In fact, many consultants spend their whole career consulting for one main client.

You want this to happen. Working with repeat clients means you already have a relationship. They don't have to evaluate you like a new hire, because they know you can deliver. You don't have to learn a new company's culture and processes, because you're already familiar with them. Everything is easier.

From a repeat client's perspective, you're reliable, already up to speed, and have a track record of success. In a word, you've become **indispensable** to your client.

That relationship is the closest thing to job security you'll find as a consultant, and developing it only requires you to do one thing: **To become indispensable, you have to become the expert in your field.**

If you're just a warm body that can operate the software or process your client uses, you might be able to find work, but you'll be easy to replace.

But if you know everything there is to know about your client's company—both the industry they're in and the specifics of their organization—then you have something they can't just replace. You have *expertise*, and expertise makes you extremely hard to replace.

I'm going to walk you through how you can become indispensable to your client by becoming an expert. It all comes down to understanding three key ideas.

1. EXPERTISE REQUIRES INTEREST

You can't be an expert in a field you aren't interested in. It's that simple.

The science on this is very clear: people will put in much more effort, and be much more effective, when working on things they enjoy. Because being an expert requires constant learning, you must pick a field you *like* learning about.

If you don't, you'll dread your work, you won't do a good job, you won't put in the right effort, and you won't ever become a real expert. Or, even worse—you'll become an expert in a field you hate. Who wants to do that?

This is one of the reasons why it's so important to clearly define your niche according to what interests you.

HOW CAN YOU APPLY THIS TO YOUR LIFE?

If you already have a niche and love your niche, that's great, consider yourself lucky and skip over this section.

Most of us are not in that situation. But that's OK, you can find a niche that is interesting to you.

Before you even think about landing consulting jobs, audit yourself thoroughly and honestly. Don't start by asking yourself what field seems the most lucrative; ask yourself three questions instead:

1. List out *everything* you are interested in. Make this list by asking yourself the following questions. Don't worry about lining these up with work subjects yet. Think about this stuff in the broadest terms possible, give yourself the most room to explore.
   a. What general subjects am I interested in?
   b. What do I read about in my free time?
   c. What problems do I like to solve?
   d. What do I want to learn about?

2. Look at that list and ask yourself honestly, "What am I good at?" Make another list of those marketable skills you know you have.
3. Now the final question: Is there a combination of a subject you enjoy and a marketable skill that fits into a legitimate business niche?

The combinations you have left once you answer question 3 are the topics you can become an expert in and can be your field.

Using myself as an example again, let's break down my list:

1. **What general subjects am I interested in?** Oil and natural gas. (No seriously, I really do *love* learning about this fascinating industry. I see it as foundational to our current standard of living, and I love the complexity of the technology and geopolitics that impact it.)
2. **What do I read about in my free time?** Business news and the energy sector (also, Texas Longhorns football).
3. **What problems do I like to solve?** I like executing difficult projects that create value and productivity for companies—and impact lots of people.
4. **What do I want to learn about?** What's going on in global business and politics, and specifically what macrotrends are impacting the oil and gas business.

Looking at that list, it's clear that I need to be involved in the oil and natural gas business. Now I have to ask myself what I'm good at that people in that industry will pay me for. To do that, I break down my relevant skills:

1. **Business strategy.** I've spent years working in and studying business, particularly as it relates to oil and natural gas, and I know how to plan for success.
2. **Team management.** I know how to put people together and get the best results from them, and I'm a natural servant leader.
3. **IT solution implementation.** Microsoft 365, SharePoint, Salesforce, trading and risk management systems—if it's a relevant piece of software to the industry, I'm interested in it and know how to implement it for the whole company.

Looking at that those skills, and comparing them to my interests, it's clear that I should be focused on developing my expertise as it relates to **project management** for the oil and gas industry.

Becoming an expert in this world isn't hard for me, because it's what I *want* to be doing with my time.

2. EXPERTISE HAPPENS THROUGH EXPERIENCE

Despite what you heard in school, formal education does little to make you an expert on anything. You can take a course and become *knowledgeable* on a subject, but there's a difference between being knowledgeable and being an expert.

Being knowledgeable means you have very specific knowledge about a subject that makes you *functional*. For example, if you took a course on commodities, you'd learn the basics of how to work in that industry. But no one would call you an expert. Similarly, an engineering degree doesn't prepare you to drill seven miles deep under the ocean floor for Chevron.

Being an expert means you have a **mastery** of your subject, and mastery only comes with experience.

Using the commodities example again, an expert would know how to handle every real-world situation that arose—and if they didn't, they'd know how to learn quickly.

Faced with a crisis, an expert wouldn't reference a case problem they worked in college, they'd think back to a similar crisis they'd seen before.

The only way to acquire this experience is by getting out into the wild. You develop a mastery of a subject by living and breathing it, not by taking a course on it.

HOW CAN YOU APPLY THIS TO YOUR LIFE?

Wherever you are in your career, you can always get more experience.

If you're an experienced consultant with years under your belt, find someone above you in your field and make them your mentor. No matter how many years you've spent in your industry, someone who has been around longer than you and has worked their way higher than you has experience they can share. If you develop a good enough relationship, they'll even become a resource you can use when you face new crises (see what I said before about knowing how to learn quickly).

If you're a young consultant just starting out, I have slightly different advice for you: Pick a field you want to be in, and then take **any** job in it. Even if you have to take less money (or significantly less money). If you work two years in an entry-level job in your chosen field, learning skills that apply to what you want to do, you'll be two years ahead of someone with an MBA. You'll have not just hands-on experience, but you'll have spent time meeting and working in front of senior people from your industry.

Senior-level professionals are much more likely to take you under their wing if they've seen your work ethic and they have some working relationship with you. They don't care what school you went to. Trust me, I hire lots of people and so do my clients. One of the biggest misconceptions is how important your university is. Nobody cares after you are twenty-five years old.

3. EXPERTISE NEVER STOPS

I started my career at Arthur Andersen, a firm renowned for the way they developed their talent. During my first performance review, I asked "What's the one thing I can do to go to the next level?"

I got a very simple response, which changed my entire life. They told me to get a subscription to *The Wall Street Journal*. I was shocked.

They knew that I needed to immerse myself in the world of business and develop a real feel for how it works, for how one thing affects another in the business world. It was one of the biggest steps forward I took as a consultant.

But I didn't stop as soon as I'd developed that feel. The world kept changing, and there was always more relevant information for me to find. To this day I read everything I can.

Every day, I pick up a new bit of information, or just further develop my feel for the way businesses work. I'm using myself as example, but this is what I see other successful consultants and contractors doing.

Here's another way of thinking through this. If you were an expert in the technology sector in 2007, you probably thought the following:

→ BlackBerry had a great position in the mobile phone market.

→ HD-DVD was going to grow and compete with Blu-ray.

→ Twitter was just a neat idea for a niche audience.

Fast forward to now. No one you know owns a BlackBerry, HD-DVD is all but gone, and Twitter has a market cap of around $10 billion.

The point is, expertise is a fluid, changing thing. There is always more to learn, and the only way to stay on top is to keep moving

HOW CAN YOU APPLY THIS TO YOUR LIFE?

Get yourself some newsfeed software. Personally, I use Google News, but you can use Feedly or whatever newsfeed you prefer. You want to compile your information from a few sources:

1. Major news outlets
2. Industry-specific outlets/trade publications
3. Stock reports and analysis from your industry
4. Thought leaders and experts in your field

When I have time throughout my day or before I go to bed, I check my feed and read everything that has been published that day. I don't tell myself, "Today I'm going to learn about shale oil." I plan every day to learn whatever I can about my industry.

One day, that might mean I read a new stock analysis of a major oil company and get some better insights into their inner workings and plans for the future. On another day, I might read about emerging technology in the field or macroeconomic trends that could potentially affect the industry.

Because I'm so deeply entrenched in all of this information—and most importantly, *I like* learning about it—I become an expert without really trying to. That's the only way to become an expert.

LESSON 3: SKILLS THAT ARE ALWAYS IN DEMAND

This section is broken into two sections:

1. Skills that are permanently in demand
2. Skills for the next five years

Let's start with the first.

SKILLS THAT ARE PERMANENTLY IN DEMAND

After working on projects for over fifteen years, I've seen certain skills that are perennially important for companies. Adding any of these skills to your résumé will virtually guarantee your ability to land work.

These skills are as follows:

1. **Great communication skills.** Companies are always looking for marketing consultants who can communicate the right messages to the right audiences. This need will never go away.

2. **Project management.** The ability to successfully execute a project is the foundation of a successful business, especially at the corporate level.

3. **Business analyst skills.** Every business needs someone who can break down their models and provide an analytical summary of where they are as a company.

4. **Strong Excel/PowerPoint skills.** PowerPoint and Excel are the key pieces of software that all corporate business runs through. Any presentation or data manipulation is going to involve these two pieces of software, and being an expert at them both makes you valuable.

5. **SAP development.** SAP is the third largest software company in the world, and the SAP ERP provides the backbone to most major corporations' technology stack.

6. **SharePoint development.** SharePoint is Microsoft's content management system, and it is used by the majority of major corporations

in the world. They have a constant need for people who can develop solutions within the platform.

7. **Process engineers.** Any business that manufactures a product consumers buy (so, most corporations) need people who can create new processes and optimize existing ones that ultimately lead to the fulfillment of a consumer's need.

8. **Java/C++/.NET developers.** These are the three development languages/frameworks most commonly used in the development of software for major corporations, and anyone who can develop in them is valuable to most corporations.

9. **Accounting/finance expertise.** Businesses are vehicles to creating money, and if you're an expert at handling that money, you're valuable to any business.

Any of these skills will make it exponentially easier for you to find work, given that they fall within your chosen niche.

SKILLS FOR THE NEXT FIVE YEARS

There are other skills that may not have the perennial power of those in the preceding list but that are going to be incredibly value for the next five years. These skills include:

1. **WorkDay experience.** WorkDay is a piece of software that is quickly becoming the standard for HR and accounting, and businesses are in dire need of people who can implement it.

2. **Saleforce.com experience.** Salesforce is the de facto sales software used by businesses today.

3. **Cyber security.** A new age of Internet has ushered in a new age of Internet crime, and businesses are in need of people who can help protect them against it.

4. **Cloud migration experience.** Whatever cloud server a corporation uses, they need someone who can migrate their data over to it without losing it.

5. **Office 365 experience.** Office 365 is the new cloud-based version of Microsoft Office, and as companies transition to it, they need experts who can transition massive teams without data loss.

6. **Marketing automation experience.** Marketo, HubSpot, and a few other key pieces of marketing automation software have become standard technology for major corporations.

Any of these skills will make you a hot commodity over the next five years.

LESSON 4: TOP TAX-SAVINGS TIPS

When I first began consulting, I did not have anyone coaching me on the financial side. I left more money on the table in the form of taxes than I care to think about, but as a result, I've learned every possible tactic to saving money on taxes as an independent consultant.

On the most basic level, you should be writing all of the following off as business expenses:

1. **Electronics.** Televisions, laptops, tablets, cell phones, and so on. Even if you also use them for personal reasons, they are a part of your work toolkit and can be written off.
2. **Office space.** Even if you work out of your own home, carve off some office space, divide the square footage from your mortgage, and pay yourself that much money in rent. That can be written off.
3. **Health insurance.** Your insurance policy is a business expense.
4. **Office supplies.** Pens, pencils, notebooks, tape—whatever you use around your office, it can add up in price over the course of a year and be a nice tax write-off.
5. **Car payment.** If you drive for work, your car is a business expense and should be taxed as such. This includes the gas you need to fill your car up and maintenance on the vehicle.

Along with these basic tips, there are some more complicated ways to save on taxes, particularly around retirement planning.

If you make up to $200,000 a year, you should set up a SEP IRA. This is an investment vehicle specifically set up for self-employed people, in which you can deposit the lesser of either 25 percent of your compensation or $54,000 tax free each year.

If you make over $200,000, you should look into setting up a defined benefits plan. A defined benefits plan is a complicated structure you will need a professional to set up for you, but in general, it creates a pension for all employees of your company in which you can save hundreds of thousands of dollars tax free.

Because you're the only employee of your company, the math works out pretty well for you.

Outside of retirement planning, you might also consider hiring your spouse or children on, even in nominal roles, to pay them salaries. Because they presumably make less than you, the income you pay out to them will be taxed at a lower bracket than it would be if you took it yourself.

CONCLUSION

We are witnessing a convergence of changes that are revolutionizing the way we think about employment and, more generally, work itself.

The thirty-year job is dying, and in its place, a new economy is rising. In this new economy, professionals are independent, free to contract for as many clients as they like, at the bill rate they choose. We are transitioning to an economy of consultants.

Does that scare you? For many people, the idea of full time, salaried employment going away forever is terrifying. But why? If you could improve your career today, what would those improvements look like?

→ **Would you want more money?** Consulting keeps you from trading your time for a salary. You can set a high hourly bill rate, get paid for every hour you work, and pay far less in taxes as an independent business than you do as a W2 employee.

→ **Would you want control over your life?** As a consultant, you take on as many—or as few—clients as you like, and set your schedule at the beginning of your contract. If you can't work past 2:00 p.m., you can set that expectation with clients and live by it.

→ **Would you want to grow faster?** If you want to change industries or specialties as a consultant, you just change your niche. It takes an afternoon to update your résumé, give your website a facelift, and adjust your BenchWatch profile.

Everything you dislike about your career is alleviated by a switch to consulting. Many people fear losing the stability they associate with full time jobs, but is that stability legitimate? Anyone old enough to be in the workforce currently was alive to see the almost nine million jobs lost between 2008 and 2010 in America. Even before the thirty-year job began its death spiral, it was not the safe bet people assumed it to be.

Consulting, conversely, is actually more stable. You aren't reliant on a single client as a consultant, and you are free to pick up new contracts as needed.

Behind this revolution are three major macroeconomic trends.

FLEXIBLE WORKFORCE SOLUTIONS

Companies simply don't want to hire full time employees anymore, and why would they? Employees are a high-ticket, constant expense that make companies less adaptable and less flexible. Full time employees are also just unnecessary for the majority of roles in an organization.

The only people who need to be salaried are the people controlling the entire company: managers, executives, people who make high-level strategic decisions and are directly responsible for the company's overall success.

People executing a specific project, on the other hand, have no real reason to be full time employees. Companies have realized that paying a consultant a higher rate per hour actually saves them money and reduces their vulnerability to changing markets.

Companies as a result are adopting flexible workforce solutions at a rapid-fire pace, which is why the already $400+ billion consulting industry is on pace to hit $450 billion (and higher) in the coming years.

However, while the consulting industry is growing at remarkable speed, it also undergoing its own radical transformation.

THE DEATH OF THE GIANT FIRM

Consulting has, for a very long time, been dominated by behemoth firms that employ tens of thousands of employees across the world. These firms have positioned themselves as one-stop shops for any business dilemma a company might face.

Need help with an acquisition, marketing, technology implementation, or project execution? You can get it all from one giant firm. Major firms, as a result, have been able to lock clients into huge, sprawling contracts, assigning dozens of junior "generalist" consultants to client projects and charging top dollar for work that is hardly top quality.

However, clients have gotten tired of this dynamic. They don't want one firm that can do everything pretty well; they want firms that can do one specific thing better than anyone else. Smaller, specialized firms can deliver that at a lower price because of their reduced overhead—they don't need office space or to pay full time salaries. As a result, small firms have risen up to become major players in the consulting world.

As the consulting industry explodes, major firms like Accenture are going to become less relevant, and small firms who contract independent consultants are going to be the new standard.

INDEPENDENT CONSULTING IS EASIER THAN EVER

The final hurdle that had to be overcome for this revolution to happen was this: professionals had to be able to become independent consultants easily. The key to this has been the development of new technology.

Registering as an independent business used to take weeks, require legal counsel, and generally be a minefield for a professional to navigate. Now, using LegalZoom, professionals can get set up as a business in a few hours.

Landing contracts as an independent consultant also used to be incredibly difficult without the client base of a major firm. Now, with platforms like BenchWatch, the entire process is smooth and approachable.

Marketing, invoicing, accounting—all of these things used to be stressful, cumbersome tasks that required a team of professionals and support staff. Now, you can use software and the occasional contractor to handle them easily and effectively.

At this point, there is only one barrier between you and an amazing career as a consultant: **Your willingness to make the leap.**

This book is your road map to taking that leap and enjoying greater wealth, stability, and growth than you've ever had in your full time job. You just have to want to do it, and then execute.

ABOUT THE AUTHOR

 **JONATHAN DISON** has spent his whole career as a consultant, having started at Arthur Andersen Consulting before going independent and growing his own firm. He is trusted by some of the world's largest companies to execute complex, strategic projects, and he has helped hundreds of people transition into consulting. Jonathan's consulting expertise has been cited by notable publications such as *Bloomberg*, *Businessweek*, the *Financial Times*, *NPR*, the *Houston Chronicle*, the *San Francisco Chronicle*, and *Oil & Gas Financial Journal*. He is also a cofounder of Bench-Watch, a service that provides education and engagement to professional consultants and helps them get discovered by consulting firms and clients.